What Happened Was:

Anna Leahy

Harbor Editions
Small Harbor Publishing

Cover art by Stacy Russo
Cover design by Taylor Blevins
Book layout by Allison Blevins and Hannah Martin

WHAT HAPPENED WAS:
ANNA LEAHY
ISBN 978-1-7359090-2-8
Harbor Editions,
an imprint of Small Harbor Publishing

CONTENTS

What Happened Was: my mother was pregnant with me   /   9

A Thousand Suns   /   10

What Happened Was: we met at a party   /   11

In the Meantime   /   12

The Center That Does Not Hold   /   13

What Happened Was: I was at a party at a fraternity house   /   14

Sheets   /   15

Gloss   /   16

What Happened Was: we worked alone together   /   17

What Happened Was: I had good news   /   18

Depth Charge   /   19

What Happened Was: cause & effect   /   20

What Happened Was: I said a goal aloud   /   22

What Happened Was: the text messages showed up on my phone   /   23

Chain Reaction   /   25

If Walls Could Talk   /   26

What Happened Was: not my story to tell   /   27

This Is Just To Say   /   28

Solve for x   /   29

What Happened Was: _____   /   31

Notes   /   33

Acknowledgments   /   34

What Happened Was:

WHAT HAPPENED WAS: MY MOTHER WAS PREGNANT WITH ME

What happened was   my mother was pregnant with me
                                 she mapped a way through without stopping

What happened was   the dean thought she would stop
                                 the dean wanted her to go away, he expected her to go away
                                 the dean said that she might fall down the stairs
                                 the dean made his secretary call to tell my mother this
                                 he would not tell her himself
                                 she was not worth his time
                                 she was expected to lose her way in this world

What happened was   my mother finished a semester late
                                 she wore a graduation robe with three velvet stripes on each sleeve   *doctorate*
                                 she held my months-old self for a photo, proof this could be done
                                 she passed the bar exam the next year, a year late

What happened was   my mother told me that life wasn't fair
                                 my mother wrote fairness into the law for me

What happened was   my mother told me that other children needed her as much as I did
                                 my mother had her own white phone on the wall for their emergencies

What happened was   my mother knew she didn't have chances others did
                                 my mother knew that she had chances others didn't

What happened was   I grew up believing in fairness and chance

A THOUSAND SUNS

Because each was as bright as the Sun,
men cowered, backs to blast:

> *Easy,* and it is and it isn't, like a gasp
> > in free fall, air held like breath, then
> > > release, atmosphere gives up, gives out.

> *Sugar* arrives with a sublime taste
> > of proximity, as between petal and stalk.

> *Fox,* as if Blake's heaven and hell rise together
> > against the dark expanse of universe.

> *How* like a haze, glowing,
> > as if through cataracts, the suggestion
> > > of *what* and *why.*

> *Climax,* the throb, the push,
> > the convex meets the concave in kilotons.

> *Moth* like insect to bulb, simple, burst and burn.

> *Stokes,* a star waking, reddening its wake,
> > growing still, the same loud hush rushes.

> *Hornet,* the larva uncurls from its corona.

We began with one, like something divine.
Why not a thousand splendors across the shadowed stretches?

WHAT HAPPENED WAS: WE MET AT A PARTY

What happened was

we met at a party
we left together
I did not mind the company
I did not care whether it was him or someone else or no one

What happened was

he suggested his girlfriend join us

What happened was

I wondered whether she sent him to parties with this in mind
I wondered why he had not suggested going back to their place
I wondered whether he had suggested a threesome to other women
I wondered who said yes

What happened was

the stories I wrote in my head to answer these questions were
much more interesting than he was

What happened was

I did not want his girlfriend to join us
I did not want to feel her absence
I did not want him to compare us
I did not want to feel like a substitute for her
I told him I was not interested

What happened was

he assumed I had been interested in him
he did not see my lack of interest as a lack of interest in him
he thought any woman who wanted to have sex wanted to have sex with him
he thought virginity explained my sudden lack of interest
he could not imagine any other reason I would turn him down
I know this because he told me so

What happened was

I wanted him to doubt himself for just a minute
but he couldn't

IN THE MEANTIME

is the mean
time, that malicious wait-and-see,
more-or-less, in-between
time, until we set our clocks back
to save the grieving daylight.

THE CENTER THAT DOES NOT HOLD

middling: Moderate or a in size, amount, or va (of a person) in reasonably not perfect he

Your life's middling, at best. At worst, it's middling too.   [*both/and*]   Manage the middle; hit your average. You're not happy and want to change your horse, your convictions.   [*neither/nor*]   You raise the finger. You feel mean. The middle has a long tail and so many choices that go nowhere.

You're stuck in it. No middle ground. All middle ground. Life's playing its ends against you. You're having a rough go of it; it's beastly. Someone says, it beats the alternative. Smack (dab)—in the middle of nowhere. Like your heart. *Thump.*

You try to change your tune, strike a chord tympanic—   [*entryway : vestibule :: exit : vertigo*]   —hammer against anvil, foot in stirrup.

You're blood-dull and falling apart. You're about to split.

tympanic:
- relating to or having tympanum (insect eardrum on the leg)
- resembling or acting like a drum head

13

WHAT HAPPENED WAS: I WAS AT A PARTY AT A FRATERNITY HOUSE

What happened was   I was at a party at a fraternity house
I had been to many parties at this fraternity house
I knew the men in this fraternity house

What happened was   probably not what you think

What happened was   one of the men kept trying to kiss me
he had done this before at parties there when he drank enough
which was what we all did at parties there

What happened was   I asked him to leave me alone
I wandered away to get out of range
I talked with other men
I tried to avoid him
I told him, *just stop*

What happened was   he followed
he pleaded
he grabbed my arm
he leaned in close
I smelled his exhalations
he would not go away

What happened was   I put my hand on his shoulder
I repeated, *just stop*
I raised my knee to his crotch
not especially swiftly
not aggressively
rather gently, somewhat firmly

What happened was   I asked his friends why they had not pulled him away
his friends said he liked me, that was all
his friends said what I had done was too much
I asked them what I should have done instead
I gained something and lost something in that asking

SHEETS

The rain comes down crisp as if starched. Weight and gravity go over one's head, and floating becomes falling. There's a chill in the air, a prevailing wind and potential.

If opposites attract, it'll happen in a flash. The binary will never do. [*do enough* | *leave well enough alone* | *as if that were enough*]   One plies another's thread counts, over-determines warp and weft. Density is mass over volume; it's piled on. The windward facing frays the lee slope at the peak. How many intersections can one tailor into a patch of world?

An expanse creates the illusion that light, too, can be sheet. Words are vapor; sentences rely on condensation. Three sheets loosen the tongue. Check the cribbed notes at the door, cheat anyway. What precipitates conversation?

Light leads and cracks. A stroke of some kind of luck. A gap between seen and heard.   [*enough hours in the day* | *enough to sink a ship* | *enough to make angels cry*]   The shortest distance between two points   ⚡ ground and sky ⚡   is a straight line. But light's jagged. It hits a return strike—

One tucks corners and another turns the double play on a tinker's curse, evers-after, and second chances. [*distance* : *attraction* :: *time* : *velocity*]   In the eye of the storm, the beginning and the end: two points in search of the perpendicular.

GLOSS

tinker's curse: *like mischief, like wandering, almost nothing at all but not quite*

Tinkers, Evers, and Chance: *Poet Franklin Pierce Adams wrote (about baseball), "These are the saddest of possible words." They fail us, these parts of speech, parts of thought, these smallest amounts of meaning. The important thing, or so they say—these words say—is to stay busy, always, and not worry about odds or results. Take one's word; pass the word like the time of day.*

In a poem called "Romance," poet Claude McKay wrote, "Love words, mad words, dream words, sweet senseless words." To run words together is to slur. To slur is to insinuate. "Insinuate" is from the Latin meaning "to curve into." "Pejorative" takes a turn for the worse | is worse for the wear, for the weathering.

"Till the end of days," McKay wrote, and you are said to be happy then. And maybe you pretend sweetness is enough for as long as you can. The pronoun here is you, and words in the dark are like birdsongs. The day can break a person, can leave a person hanging. McKay also wrote a poem called "The Lynching." This sin so blanched it is unforgivable till the end of days.

A simple truth becomes sealed in a poem about something else. Enough is not enough.

Why all italics? This is hard to read.

WHAT HAPPENED WAS: WE WORKED ALONE TOGETHER

What happened was	we worked alone together typesetting late one night, I flirted with him to see what would happen to test whether I could seduce
What happened was	we went back to his place, his space we kissed, we fondled
What happened was	he excused himself I sat alone on the couch I still had my jacket on I grew bored I had already proved myself to myself, the proof of being there
What happened was	he returned naked he wore glasses
What happened was	maybe I laughed maybe I rolled my eyes maybe I said, *you've rushed ahead without me*
What happened was	he got dressed he said I should leave or I did
What happened was	I found a photo on a bulletin board for anyone to see my face was smashed out with a white sticky print the size and shape of his thumb

WHAT HAPPENED WAS: I HAD GOOD NEWS

What happened was   I had good news
                     I wanted to tell him my good news
                     he had already heard my good news
                     I didn't know he had heard

What happened was   I walked out of my office
                     he walked out of his office into its narrow hallway
                     I didn't know he had walked out of his office
                     I turned the corner into his narrow hallway

What happened was   he kissed me full on the mouth
                     he was happy, he was excited

What happened was   I do not remember what I said in response
                     I turned around as quickly as I politely could
                     I went down the stairs like rapid heartbeats

What happened was   I told two people, they cringed
                     as if I were looking in a mirror for my response
                     we thought he meant well or that he meant to mean well
                     we thought it was a shame he'd done this
                     I was glad no one else had seen
                     no one else knew

What happened was   I knew not to ruin the idea of him for other people
                     what good would that do

What happened was   my lips took a while for the memory to leave them

DEPTH CHARGE

Underwater, that which is most volatile
is amplified when detonated,
sending out waves of pressure
in every direction, seemingly targetless
but full like noise and intentional.
No wonder I break,
strew my compartments, and sink.
The slowness of sinking creates a new and silent
wake, a wakefulness from indirection,
a suddenly coherent sense of a location
replete with circumstance.
If *mine* were merely a possessive pronoun,
would the word
plumb this site? And then, darkness
regains its composure far from surface and shore,
still teeming with syllables left to spill.

WHAT HAPPENED WAS: CAUSE & EFFECT

What happened was   cause & effect, like ripples & dominoes & butterflies
the road to hell was well paved with intentions

What happened was   forced down the throat of this world where paper never refused ink
rape was *the carnal knowledge of a female, forcibly and against her will*
this was the definition for eighty years
the definition for my mother's entire lifetime

What happened was   I grew up in *no* means *no* & a crisis hotline number on the bathroom stall
silence was not *no, maybe* could be *yes,* depending on
who said it when in the same old he-said-she-said story
these were the oldest tricks in the old book

What happened was   both roads & tongues can be forked
a person can run out of things to say before a person runs out of road
rape is *the penetration, no matter how slight*
rape is *the vagina or anus with any body part or object*
rape is *oral penetration by a sex organ*
rape is *without the victim's consent*
this definition is not as old as the hills, not as tough as old boots
a rock to push uphill, to live under

What happened was   suddenly *yes* means *yes* for anyone's flesh, not only the forcible female
even *yes-yes-yes* can be withdrawn suddenly
like any other offer of something worth something to someone
like condolences & olive branches

What happened was   sins cast long shadows beyond a doubt, no crime in that, no body
old dogs & old bottles & old blocks still chipping off
teasing, offhand comments, isolated incidents
unwelcome advances, something for something, comments & gestures
frequent or severe, hostile or offensive
anyone might be the shadow of oneself that only the shadow knows

What happened was   a hill of beans to die on, a river to ford
I must confess to the world   *the course I took seemed the better as well as the easier*
no personal vendetta   *more comfortable to remain silent*   *I had to tell the truth*
a mountain made from molehills takes time, stands the test of it
I am terrified   *it is my civic duty to tell you what happened*
the reality has been far worse than I expected   *I have seen my life picked apart*
force of habit is a force to be reckoned with

WHAT HAPPENED WAS: I SAID A GOAL ALOUD

What happened was   I said a goal aloud
something I thought I needed or wanted to advance my career
something I had been working toward for a long time
I was full of drive, I knew where I was going
I must have looked full of doubt to him

What happened was   he was extending a version of kindness
as if not to leave me to someone's tender mercies

What happened was   he said that when he was in the room
he would advocate for me
he would do what he could
as if success were a matter of favors and
he held a bounty in his back pocket

What happened was   he didn't think I could be in the room
he didn't think I could be in the room before he was in the room
he didn't think about how much closer to the room I was
he didn't think through what he said
he didn't have to

What happened was   not important to him
not something he would remember
not worth talking about with him

What happened was   what he said didn't change anything, not really
he felt better about himself for having said it
for me, there was only going into the room before him

What happened was   he was offering me something
I was ungrateful because I didn't need it

WHAT HAPPENED WAS: THE TEXT MESSAGES SHOWED UP ON MY PHONE

What happened was   the text messages showed up on my phone
I ignored them
I thought it was a mistake
another mistake and another mistake

What happened was   the first message was from Steve
the second was from HQ, the third from Hali
the fourth said, *hey baby*
the fifth said, *Do you really just want nudes*
the sixth was in Spanish

What happened was   the twelfth said, *Stuck up bitch*
the thirteenth said, *You still wanna hook up?*
the fourteenth named the dating site
I contacted the dating site to ask that my number be removed

What happened was   there were eggplant emojis
there were photographs of penises
one said, *It's urgent*
the dating site calls this *social discovery*
the dating site says the best day for browsing is Sunday
the dating site suggests becoming an entrepreneur

What happened was   the dating site replied
Can you please ask one of the people who contacted you to provide you—
the dating site claims more than four-hundred million users
Was this answer helpful?
that answer was not helpful

What happened was   the fake account was removed

What happened was   I wonder whether a woman had mistyped my number as hers
I imagine her fingers swiping, searching
I imagine her finally seeing all those messages not meant for me
she could *get closer to who you're looking for* or further away
light-years from here, someday

CHAIN REACTION

Criticality:
and she told two people and
stray neutrons uttered.

IF WALLS COULD TALK

Speak with spray paint. Use big, confident letters, a symbol or two for clarity or conciseness, for aesthetics or effect. Shout, if you can. Use all-caps & punctuation. Or write in whispers if what you have to say is inappropriate. If you cannot say anything at all, keep your quiet in concrete. Silence is hard too. Notice the color and texture of the unsayable, wish it blue like the sky after a thunderstorm passes. Do not open your lips. Do not taste a wall. After the wall falls to pieces (as walls do because something does not love them), pick up the pieces and put graffiti in others' hands. Listen to the silent wishes people unlike and like you left there, secreted, waiting to cross over. Welcome them. Reach for them as if they are your own.

WHAT HAPPENED WAS: NOT MY STORY TO TELL

What happened was   not my story to tell
not that bad
something I could carry with me, something empty

What happened was   I went to bars
I stayed out till all hours
I walked home alone in the dark
I drove alone on highways
I went to men's apartments with them
I did not choose men wisely
I wasn't always the best version of myself
I said yes
I said no
I said maybe, let's see how it goes

What happened was   the men I knew well didn't rape me
the men I barely knew didn't rape me
men I didn't know didn't rape me

What happened was   I felt lucky
I felt grateful

What happened was   wasn't luck
wasn't something I should thank anyone for

What happened was   there are statistics
there is no formula

What happened was   as chance would have it
something slim or fat, last or even, sporting or fighting

THIS IS JUST TO SAY

after two poems about plums by William Carlos Williams

What happened seemed
like ripe plums from the icebox
not yet forbidden but
in need of forgiveness,
just turned, too
sweet, already fermenting.

What happened
seemed bad to her.
This is just to say.
What happened seemed
bad to her.

What happened seemed bad
to her. Someone said it was
not that bad
and she tasted what that meant,
so delicious, such solace,
and kept quiet.

SOLVE FOR X

for the many silence breakers

x happens for a reason
x happens for no reason
x has the power of magnification
x is a voiceless consonant cluster
x is a whisper
x is not that bad—
                        —x is worse than anyone knows
x is a sex chromosome
y is a sex chromosome—
                        —why is a question
                        —why is a response
y can be vowel or consonant, lucky that way
y is the fingers folded, the thumb and pinky extended, saying hang loose—
                        —y is the same hand tipping thumb to lips, saying drink
                        —y is the same hand with thumb to ear, pinky to lips, saying call me
y is unrestricted economy travel
                        —why buy the cow, why in the devil, why in god's name, why not
x is the horizontal axis
x marks the spot
x marks the choice in a box
x marks a place not to go
x means to cross, is a cross—
                        —x is an intersection
x is a fist with the first finger raised and crooked like a hook
x is pronounced before a syllable of stress—
                        —x can be completely silent at the end of what's said
xoxoxo—x is a kiss
x drawn over the heart is a promise of secrecy
x is drawn over something to negate it—
                        —x means no
x is a god, a sacrifice
x is infrequent
x multiplies
x has ancestors and descendants—
                        —x has history behind it and a future ahead of it

x is experimental
x is extreme
x is stimulant and hallucinogen
x is pornographic
x is a whiffed attempt and another two swings—
                              —x knocks down all the pins
x is the crosshairs marking the target
x risks death by poison
x is the generic version, the no-name
x is a letter—
                              —x is an ancient number
x creates dimensions, breadth and depth and height
x describes waves with accelerating electrons that see through the skin
x replaces one's name written in one's own hand
x hopes with fingers hidden behind the back
x is a placeholder for the unknown thing
x is an independent variable—
                              —solve for x

WHAT HAPPENED WAS: _____

What happened was _____

What happened was I grew through and around and in between it all
whatever it was—or wasn't—became me

What happened was I wrote what happened
I erased what I wrote so the page would hold only silence
I didn't want what happened to interrupt the silence of a blank page
to be contained by the space around it
I didn't want what had—or had not—happened to matter on a page
I didn't want it to be seen and not matter
I didn't want anyone to see how it didn't matter
erasure is from the Latin for *scratch* or *scrape,* like an itch or a scab

What happened was avoidance

What happened was the page made me nervous
no, the person I imagined reading the words made me nervous
my memory is unmemorable
I'm no worse for the wear of recollection
I cede that point

What happened was the blank page becomes an invitation
a space before text
a place for someone else's voice
another story
my hand cupped to my ear, I'm listening

What happened was there is room enough
it's a big page
turn the page, and there's another
turn it over in your mind
draw a blank
fill it in

NOTES

"A Thousand Suns": Italicized words are names of some of the nuclear tests conducted by the United States. The descriptions are based on photographs of nuclear tests in *100 Suns* by Michael Light. William Blake wrote and illustrated *The Marriage of Heaven and Hell*.

"The Center That Does Not Hold" is a title adapted from a line in the poem "The Second Coming" by W. B. Yeats. Other lines echo that poem as well.

"Sheets" & "Gloss" refer to Joe Tinker, Johnny Evers, and Frank Chance, who played together for the Chicago Cubs in 1902-1912 and were memorialized in Franklin Pierce Adams's poem "Baseball's Sad Lexicon." A tinker is a tinsmith and colloquially (and derogatorily) a mischievous British child or an Irish nomad, and a tinker's curse refers to something insignificant.

"What Happened Was: cause & effect": The definitions of rape are drawn from federal guidelines used by the FBI before and since 2013; legal definitions of rape vary by state. The definition of sexual harassment is adapted from EEOC guidelines. The italicized portions of the last stanza are excerpted from Anita Hill's opening statement to Congress in 1991 and Chistine Blasey Ford's opening statement to Congress in 2018.

"If Walls Could Talk" was inspired by the fall of the Berlin Wall, makes a gesture to Robert Frost's poem "Mending Wall," and suggests other walls as well.

"This Is Just to Say" shares its title with a poem by William Carlos Williams in which the speaker eats plums someone was saving for breakfast. This poem draws also from Williams's "To a Poor Old Woman," in which a woman on the street eats a plum from a paper bag.

ACKNOWLEDGMENTS

I appreciate the trust that editors of the following publications placed in my poems:

Escape Into Life: "What Happened Was: my mother was pregnant with me," "What Happened Was: I was at a party at a fraternity house," "What Happened Was: he was extending kindness," "What Happened Was: _____," and "This Is Just To Say"

Fugue: "Depth Charge"

La Fovea: "In the Meantime"

Mayo Review: "If Walls Could Talk" (as "How To Talk to a Wall")

The POWER Anthology, Public Poetry: "A Thousand Suns"

Sugared Water: "Chain Reaction" (as "Nuclear Haiku")

SWWIM: "Solve for x"

Whale Road Review: "What Happened Was: we worked alone together"

Much thanks to Harbor Editions and especially to Allison Blevins, who has shepherded these poems together into the world. Gratitude also to Stacy Russo, whose artwork "Women Gathering to Create Beauty" holds these poems.

I am grateful for Dorland Mountain Arts Colony and the Ragdale Foundation, where many of these poems found their footing, for my fellow writers and artists in these two communities, and to Chapman University for time to finish this chapbook.

Nancy Kuhl remains a trusted reader whenever I think I have more than a pile of poems; gratitude to her for helping me understand their connections. Beth Ann Fennelly, Oliver de la Paz, and Lynne Thompson offered generous words in support of this chapbook. I'm grateful that the poems of all four of these writers are in this world.

Thanks to the many family, friends, and writers who've helped me envision and sustain my writing life, especially Brigid and Maggie. Most enormous thanks to Doug.

Anna Leahy is the author of the poetry collections *Aperture* (Shearsman, 2017) and *Constituents of Matter* (Kent State UP, 2007), which won the Wick Poetry Prize, and three chapbooks, including *What Happened Was:* (Harbor Editions, 2021). She is also the author of the nonfiction book *Tumor* (Bloomsbury, 2017). Her poems and essays have appeared at *Aeon, The Atlantic, Buzzfeed, Cimarron Review, Comstock Review, Crab Orchard Review, Fifth Wednesday Journal, Poetry, The Pinch, The Rumpus, Scientific American, Southern Humanities Review, The Southern Review,* and elsewhere, and her essays have won the top awards from *Mississippi Review, Los Angeles Review, Ninth Letter,* and *Dogwood*. She directs the MFA program at Chapman University, where she edits *TAB: The Journal of Poetry & Poetics*.

See more: www.amleahy.com | @AMLeahy on Twitter | @AnnaLeahyAuthor on Facebook